Origami

The Art and Fun of
Japanese Paper Folding

FUMIAKI SHINGU

Mud Puddle inc.
NEW YORK

Origami
The Art and Fun of Japanese Paper Folding
Created by Fumiaki Shingu

© 2006 by Mud Puddle Books, Inc.

Mud Puddle Books, Inc.
36 W. 25th Street
5th Floor
New York, NY 10010
info@mudpuddleinc.com

ISBN: 978-1-60311-089-1

Printed and bound in China

Contents

Introduction

THE MAGICAL WORLD OF ORIGAMI

PICTURE A SQUARE PIECE OF PAPER.

Imagine that square piece of paper turning into an animal, a flower, a box or something that moves.

This is the timeless appeal of origami, the Japanese art of paper folding. Origami has been captivating people and holding them spellbound for more than a thousand years. It's believed that by folding, decorating and playing with paper you cultivate your creativity and spark your imagination.

It's easy to master the techniques of origami and, by practicing as much as you can, you develop your skills and quickly move on to more advanced steps and projects.

This book can be used by beginners and experts alike. The projects are classified according to their level of difficulty. Children and adults will readily find projects that match their skills.

It makes me very happy to share my origami experiences with you and I would be so pleased if my origami techniques provide you with joy and delight.

—Fumiaki Shingu
Tokyo 2006

Explanation of Diagrams

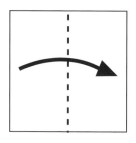 

Fold on the dotted line.

Fold backward on the dotted line.

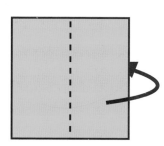 

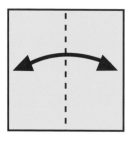 

Fold to make a crease and fold back.

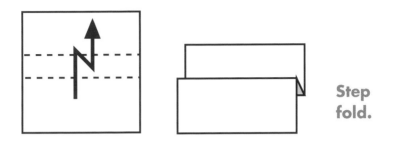

Step fold.

Turn over.

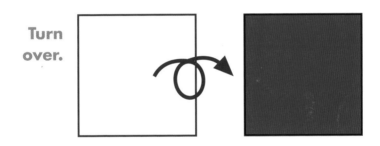

Turn around.

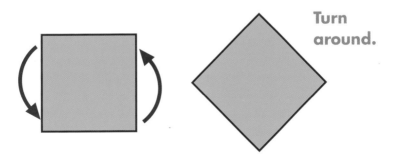

Pocket fold on the dotted line.

 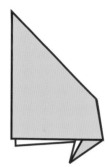

Hood fold on the dotted line.

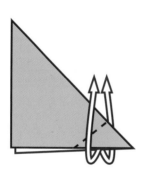 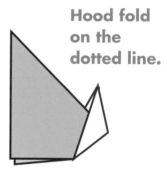

Level of Difficulty

 1 star - Very Easy

⭐⭐ 2 stars - Easy

⭐⭐⭐ 3 stars - A bit more difficult

Folding Techniques

Take time to practice and master the three basic folds described here. They are used throughout this book and will allow you to create the beautiful projects that follow.

Step Fold

❶ Fold on the dotted lines as if you were making a stair.

❷ First fold up on the dotted line.

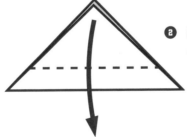

❸ Then fold back down on the other dotted line to complete the step fold.

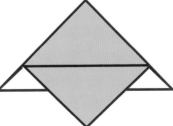

Pocket Fold

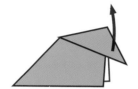

1 Fold to make a crease.

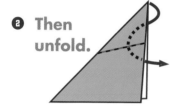

2 Then unfold.

3 Hold the top.

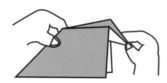

4 And tuck in.

Hood Fold

1 Fold to make a crease.

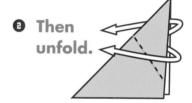

2 Then unfold.

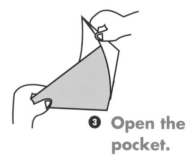

3 Open the pocket.

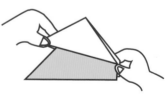

4 And fold to cover the top.

EASY

Cat Face

① Fold in half.

② Fold in half to make a crease and unfold.

③ Fold on the dotted lines.

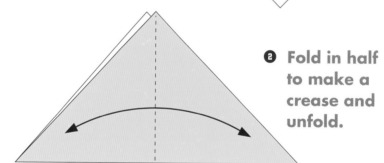

12

4 Fold on the dotted line.

5 Turn over.

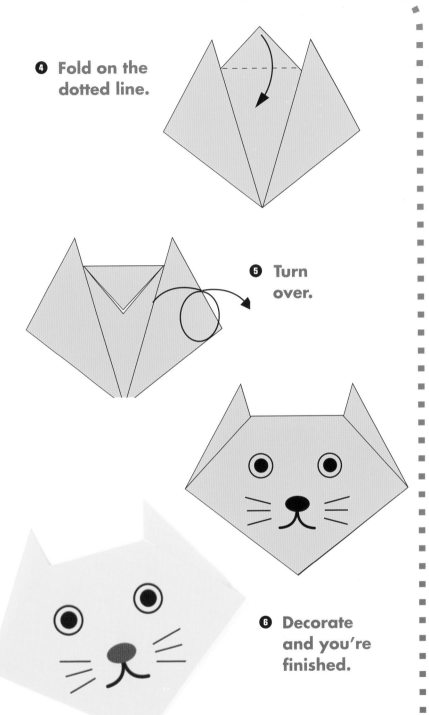

6 Decorate and you're finished.

Dog Face ⭐

❶ **Fold in half.**

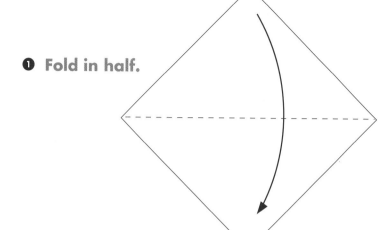

❷ **Fold in half to make a crease and unfold.**

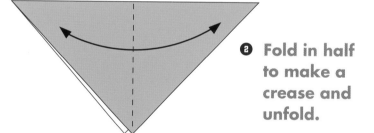

❸ **Fold on the dotted lines.**

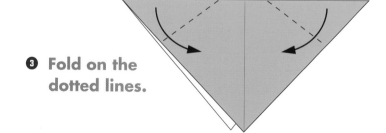

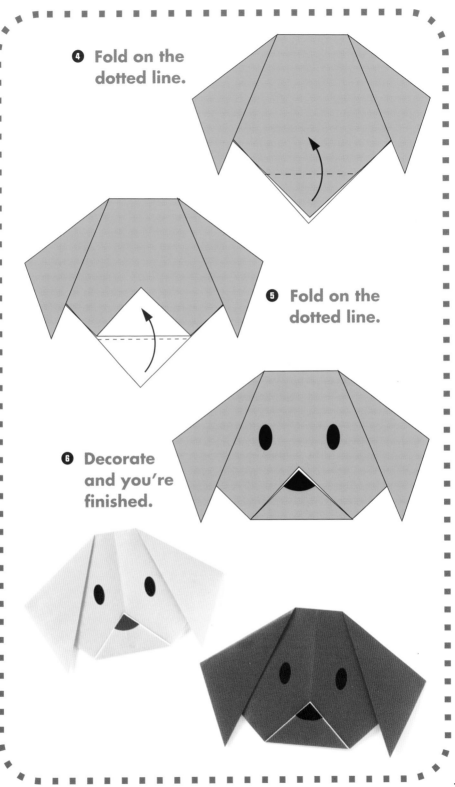

4 Fold on the dotted line.

5 Fold on the dotted line.

6 Decorate and you're finished.

FUN

Boat ★★

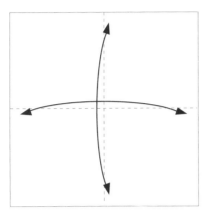

❶ Fold on the dotted lines to make creases and unfold.

❷ Fold on the dotted lines to meet the center line.

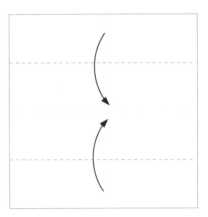

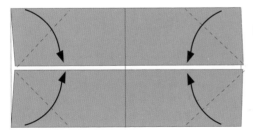

❸ Fold on the dotted lines.

❹ Fold on the dotted line.

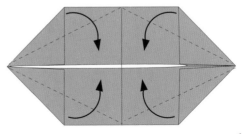

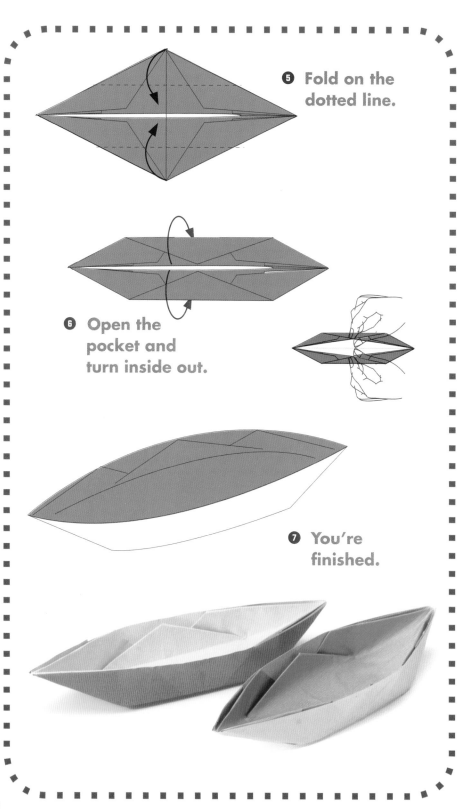

❺ Fold on the dotted line.

❻ Open the pocket and turn inside out.

❼ You're finished.

Jumping Frog

❶ Fold in half to make a crease and unfold.

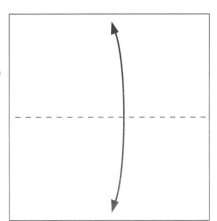

❷ Fold in half.

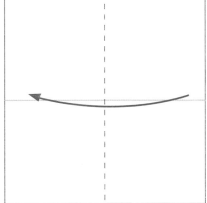

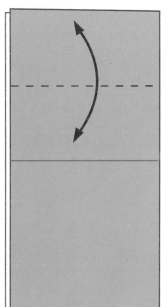

❸ Fold on the dotted line to make a crease and unfold.

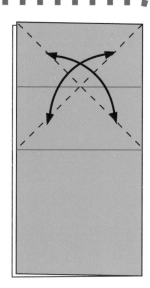

❹ Fold to make creases and unfold

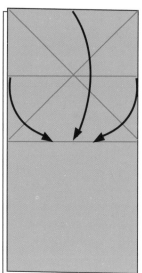

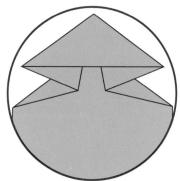

❺ Fold on the dotted lines.

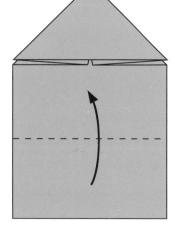

❻ Fold on the dotted line.

❼ Fold on the
dotted lines
to meet the
center line.

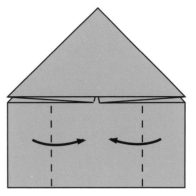

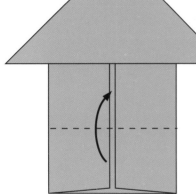

❽ Fold on the
dotted line.

❾ Fold on the
dotted line to
make a crease
and unfold.

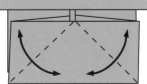

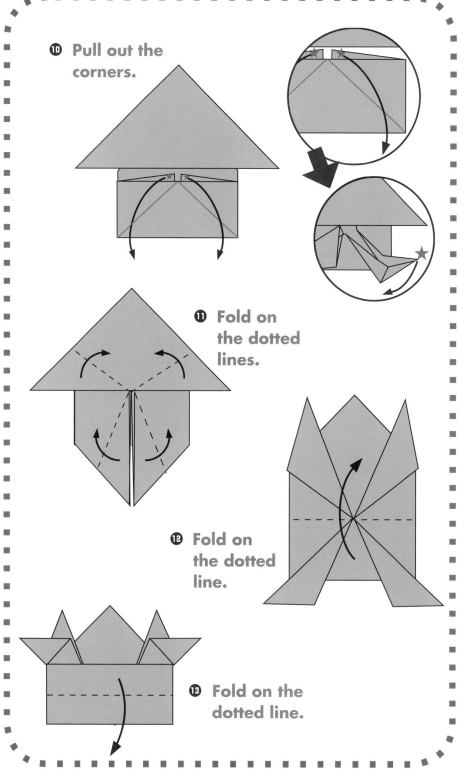

⑩ Pull out the corners.

⑪ Fold on the dotted lines.

⑫ Fold on the dotted line.

⑬ Fold on the dotted line.

⑭ Turn over.

⑮ Decorate and you're finished.

Press down with a finger and release to make the frog jump.

CREATURES

Elephant ★★★

❶ Fold in half to make a crease and unfold.

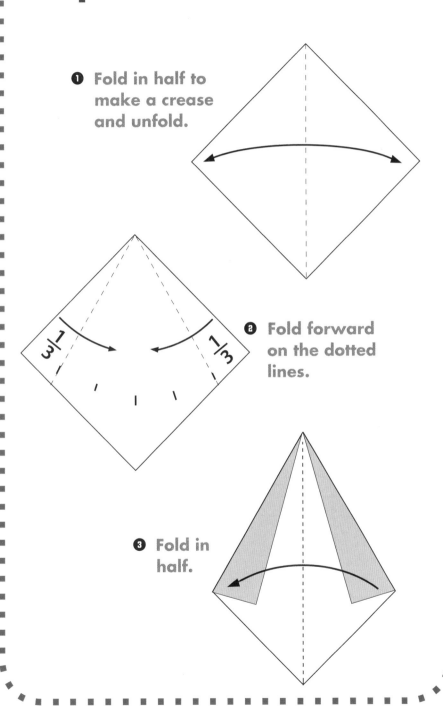

❷ Fold forward on the dotted lines.

$\frac{1}{3}$ $\frac{1}{3}$

❸ Fold in half.

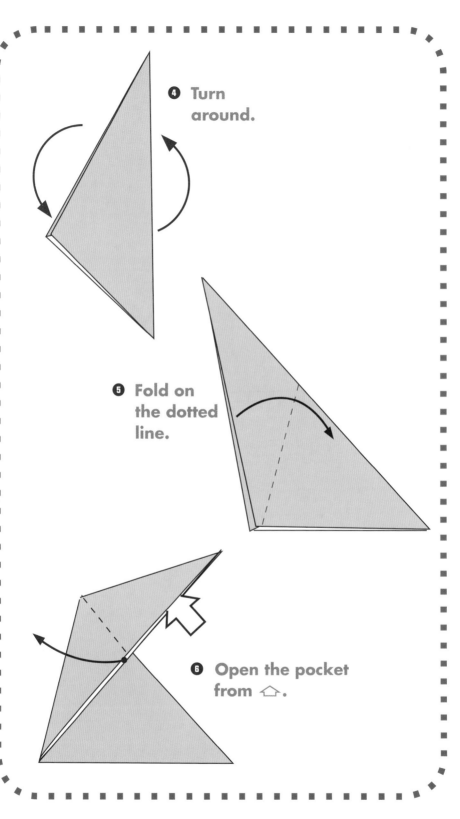

❹ Turn around.

❺ Fold on the dotted line.

❻ Open the pocket from ⌂.

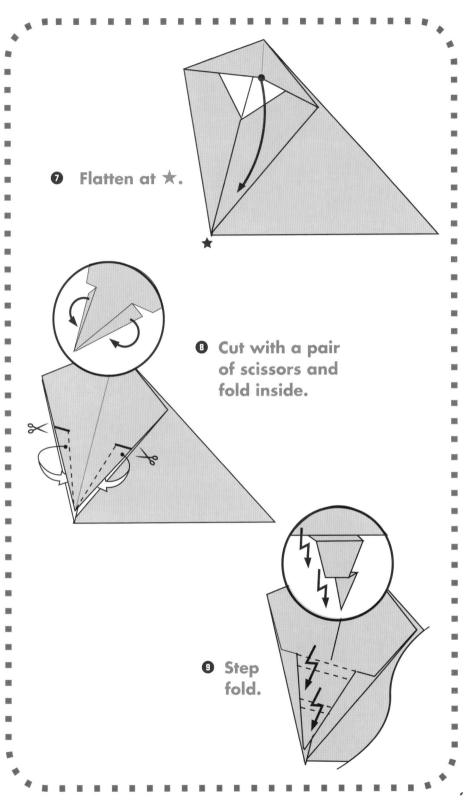

❼ Flatten at ★.

❽ Cut with a pair of scissors and fold inside.

❾ Step fold.

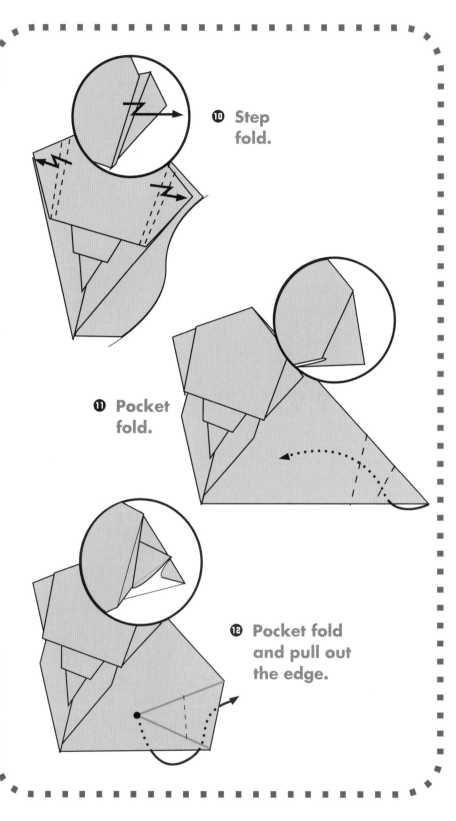

10 Step fold.

11 Pocket fold.

12 Pocket fold and pull out the edge.

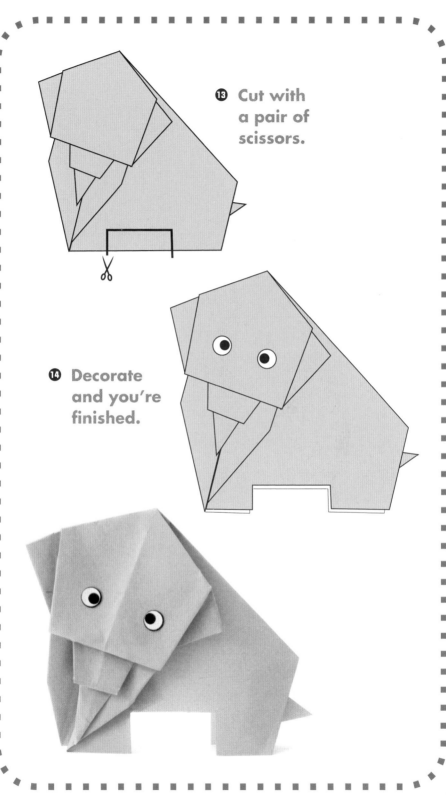

⓭ Cut with a pair of scissors.

⓮ Decorate and you're finished.

Giraffe ★★

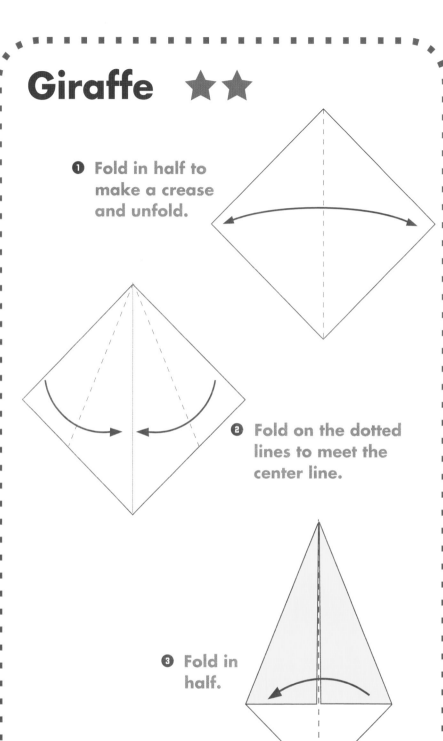

❶ Fold in half to make a crease and unfold.

❷ Fold on the dotted lines to meet the center line.

❸ Fold in half.

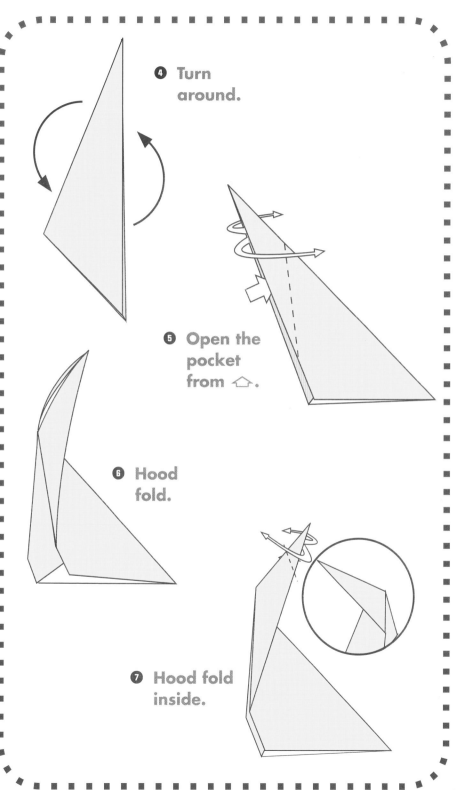

❹ Turn around.

❺ Open the pocket from ⬡.

❻ Hood fold.

❼ Hood fold inside.

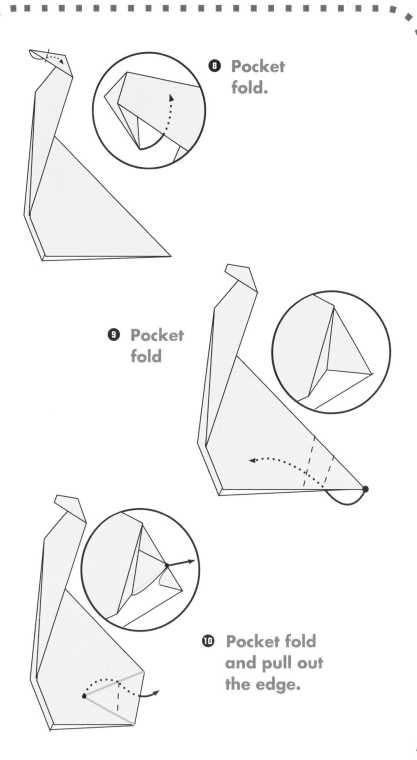

❽ Pocket fold.

❾ Pocket fold

❿ Pocket fold and pull out the edge.

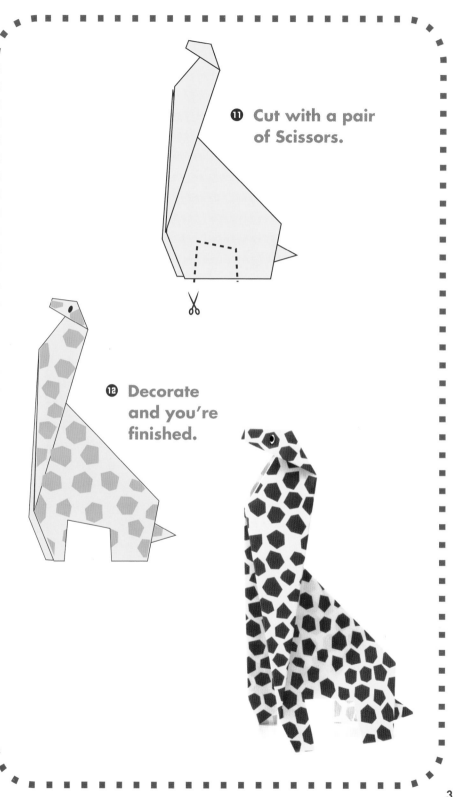

⓫ Cut with a pair of Scissors.

⓬ Decorate and you're finished.

33

Lady Bug

❶ Fold on the dotted lines to meet the center line.

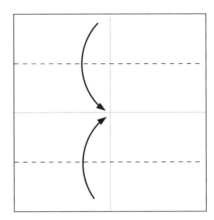

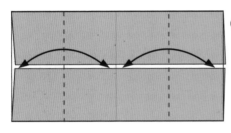

❷ Fold on the dotted lines to meet the center line and unfold.

❸ Fold on the dotted lines.

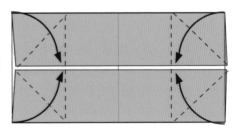

❹ **Open the pocket
from ⌂ and
flatten.**

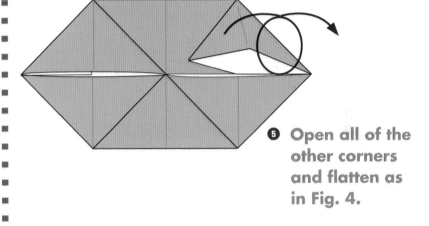

❺ **Open all of the
other corners
and flatten as
in Fig. 4.**

❻ **Fold on the
dotted lines.**

❼ Fold on the dotted lines.

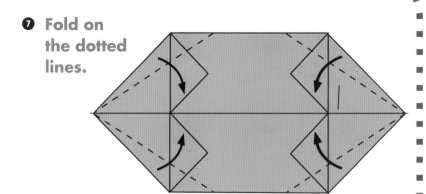

❽ Fold backward on the dotted line.

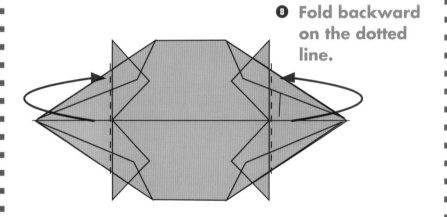

❾ Fold on the dotted line.

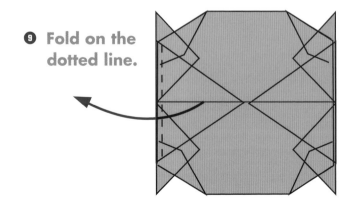

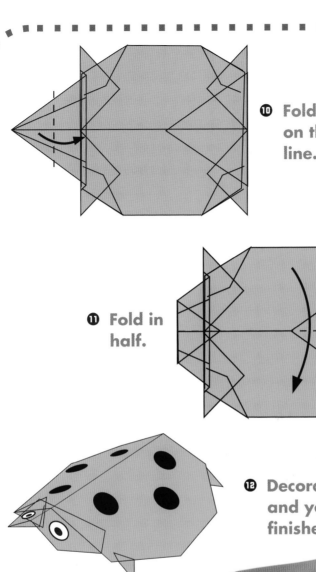

⑩ Fold backward on the dotted line.

⑪ Fold in half.

⑫ Decorate and you're finished.

Panther

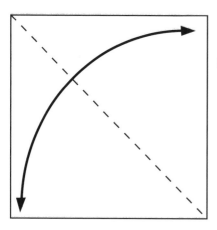

❶ Fold in half to make a crease and unfold.

❷ Fold on the dotted lines to meet the center line.

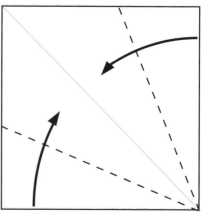

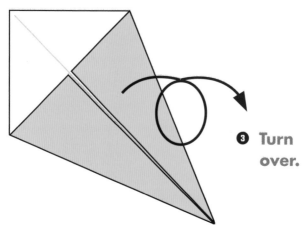

❸ Turn over.

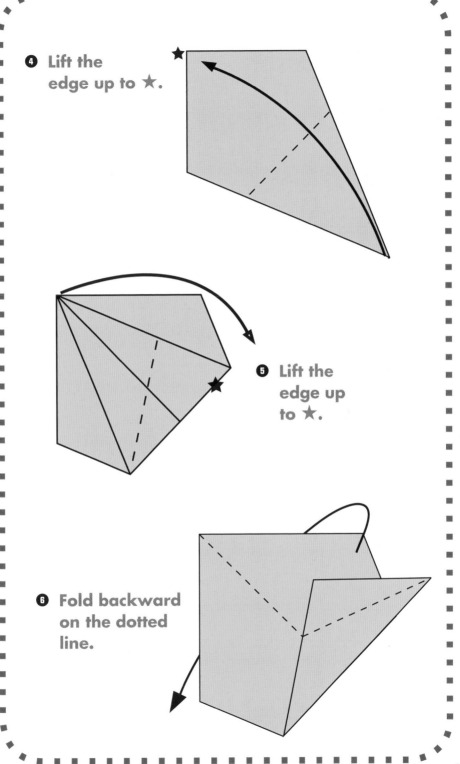

❹ Lift the edge up to ★.

❺ Lift the edge up to ★.

❻ Fold backward on the dotted line.

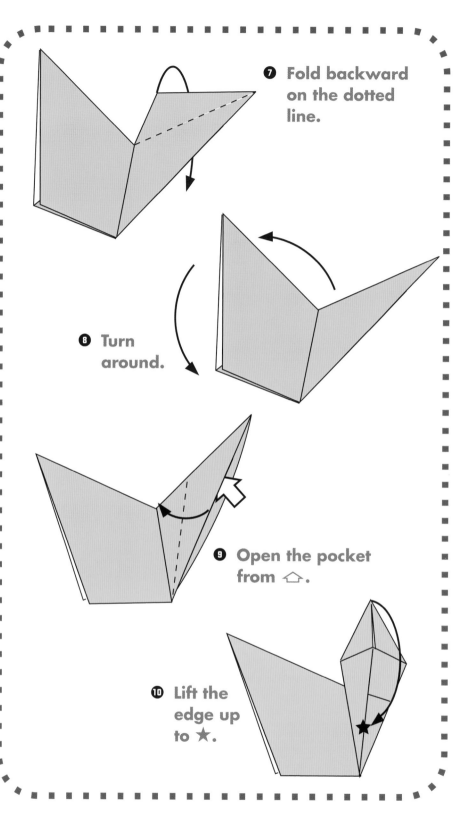

❼ Fold backward on the dotted line.

❽ Turn around.

❾ Open the pocket from △.

❿ Lift the edge up to ★.

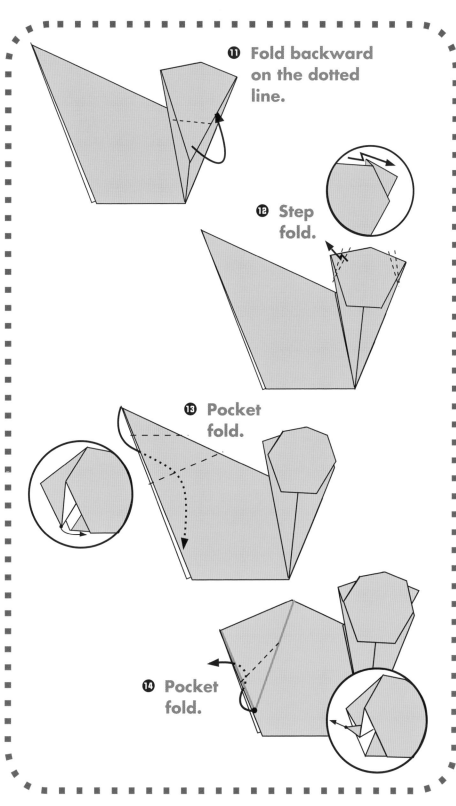

⑪ **Fold backward on the dotted line.**

⑫ **Step fold.**

⑬ **Pocket fold.**

⑭ **Pocket fold.**

⓯ Cut with a pair of scissors.

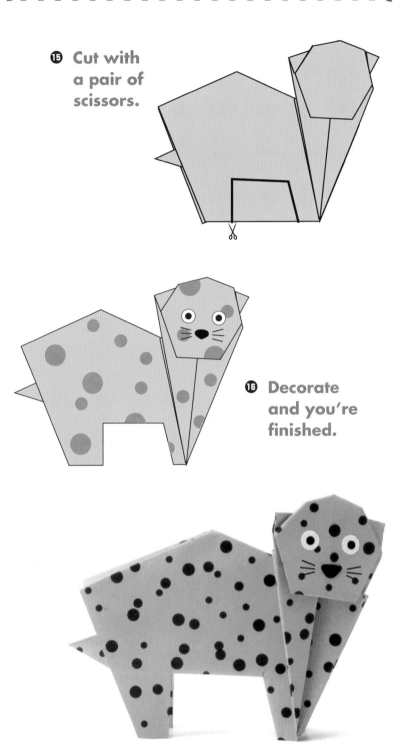

⓰ Decorate and you're finished.

Crane ★★

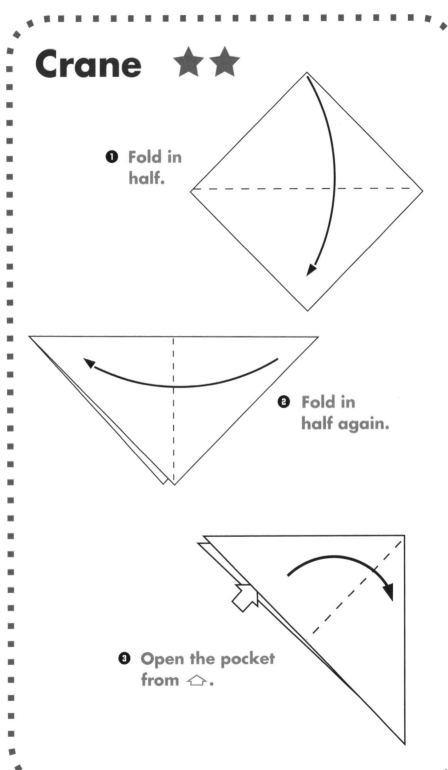

1 Fold in half.

2 Fold in half again.

3 Open the pocket from ⌂.

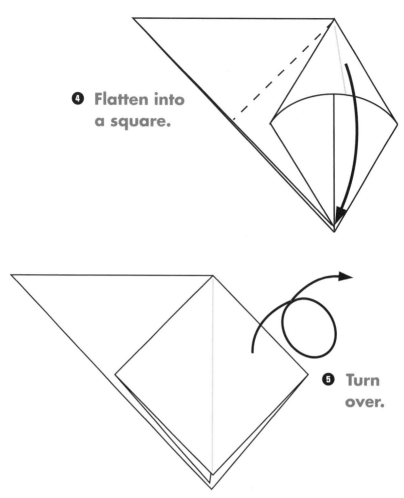

4 Flatten into a square.

5 Turn over.

6 Open the pocket from 🔺 and flatten into a square as in Figs 3 & 4.

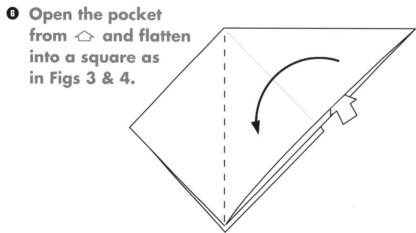

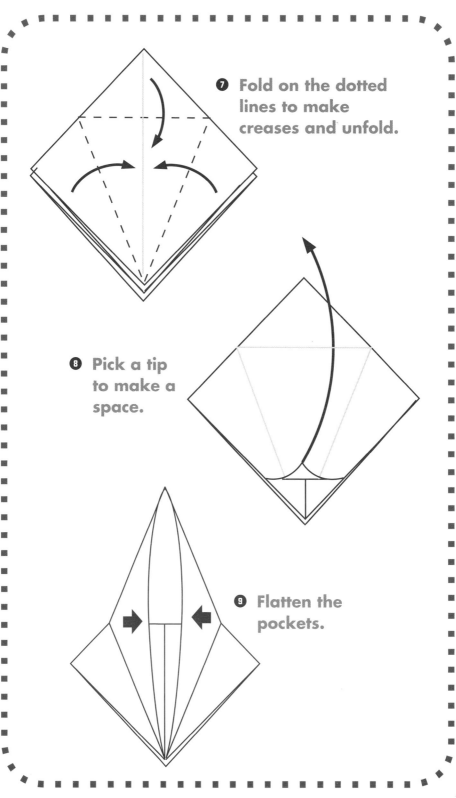

7 Fold on the dotted lines to make creases and unfold.

8 Pick a tip to make a space.

9 Flatten the pockets.

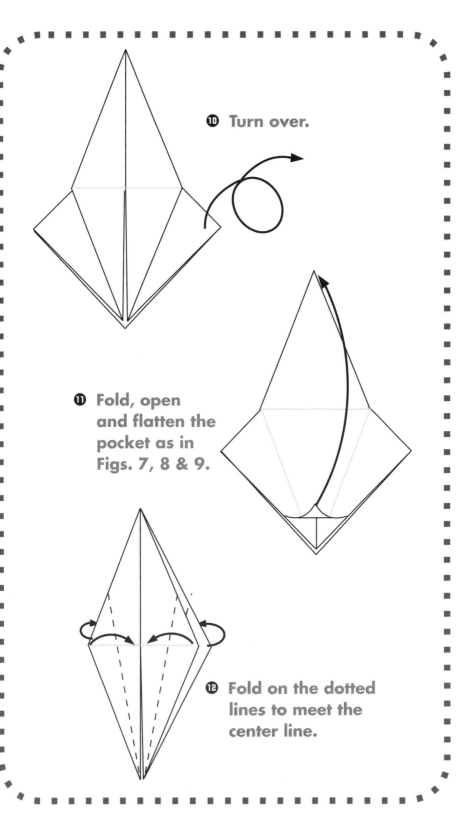

10 Turn over.

11 Fold, open and flatten the pocket as in Figs. 7, 8 & 9.

12 Fold on the dotted lines to meet the center line.

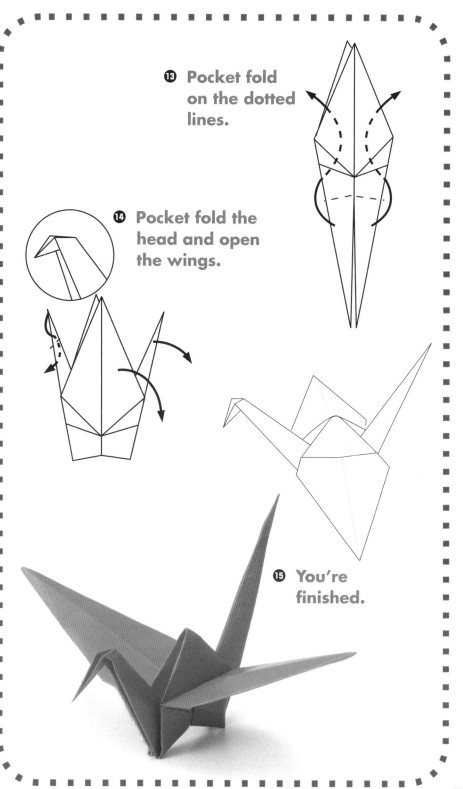

⑬ Pocket fold on the dotted lines.

⑭ Pocket fold the head and open the wings.

⑮ You're finished.

HOLIDAY

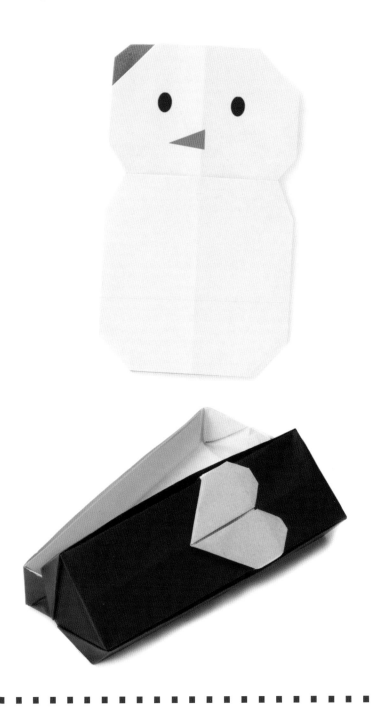

Snowman

❶ Fold in half.

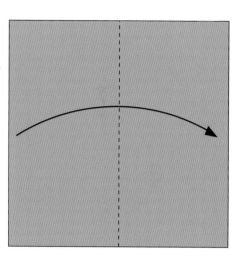

❷ Fold to make a crease and unfold.

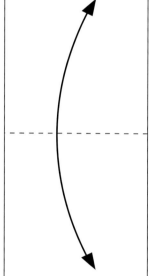

❸ Step fold forward on the dotted lines.

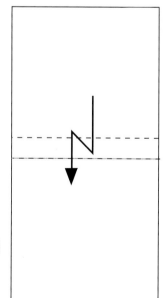

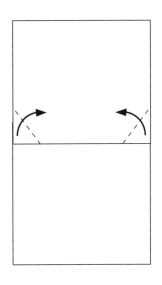

❹ Fold on the dotted line.

❺ Fold on the dotted lines.

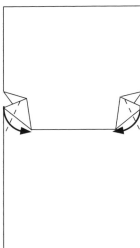

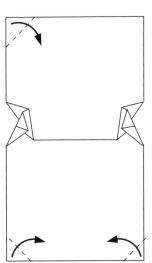

❻ Fold on the dotted lines.

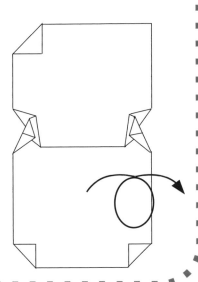

❼ Turn over.

50

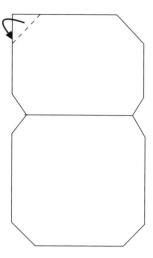 **8** Fold inside.

 **9** Fold backward on the dotted lines.

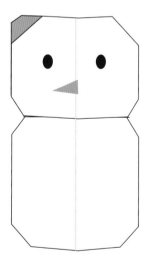 **10** Fold in half, decorate and you're finished.

Santa

❶ Fold on the dotted
line to make a
crease and
unfold.

❷ Fold on the dotted
lines to meet the
center line.

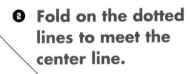

❸ Fold to make
creases and
unfold.

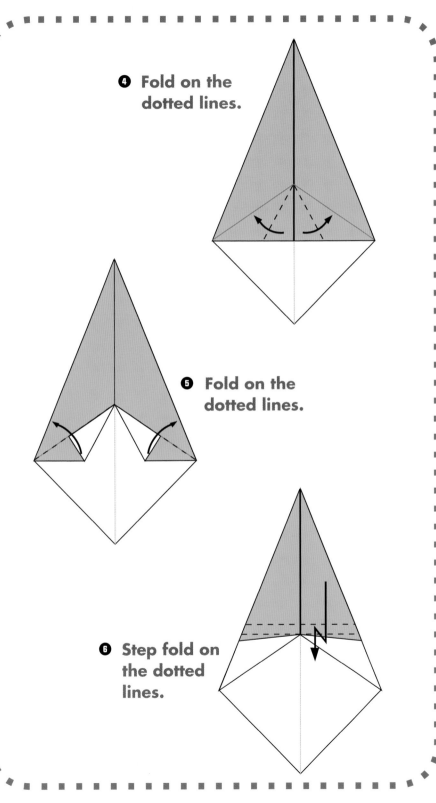

❹ Fold on the dotted lines.

❺ Fold on the dotted lines.

❻ Step fold on the dotted lines.

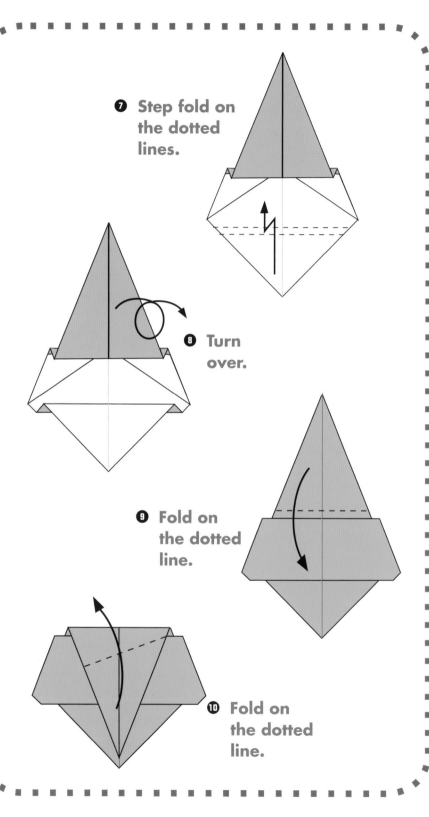

7 Step fold on the dotted lines.

8 Turn over.

9 Fold on the dotted line.

10 Fold on the dotted line.

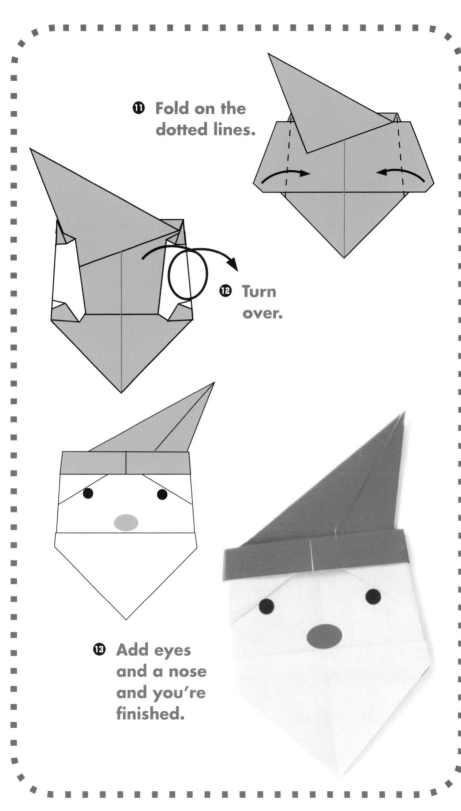

⑪ **Fold on the dotted lines.**

⑫ **Turn over.**

⑬ **Add eyes and a nose and you're finished.**

Easter Bunny

❶ Fold in half.

❷ Fold in half to make a crease and unfold.

❸ Fold on the dotted line.

56

❹ Fold on the dotted lines to meet the center line.

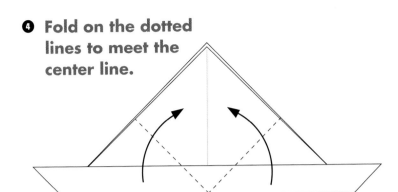

❺ Turn over.

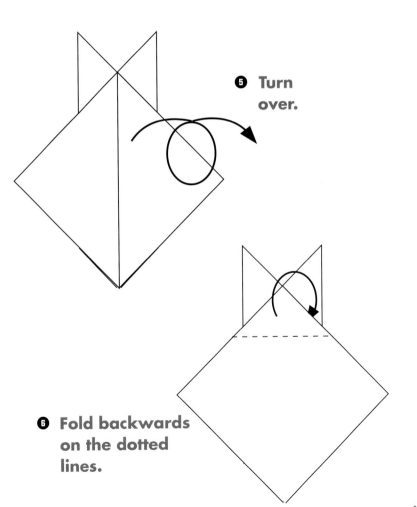

❻ Fold backwards on the dotted lines.

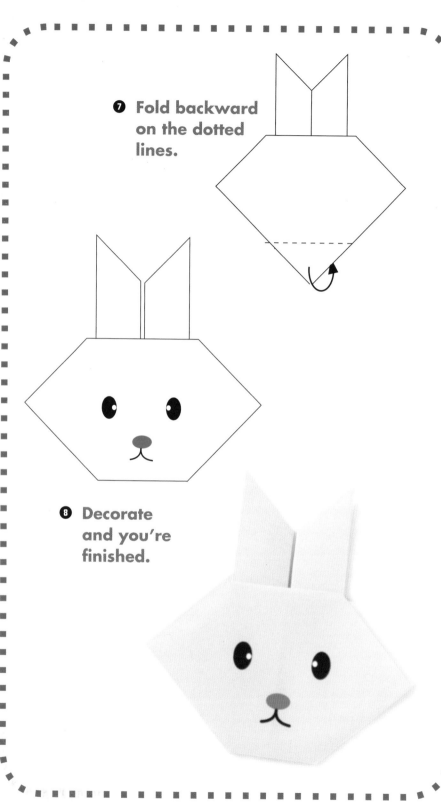

7 Fold backward on the dotted lines.

8 Decorate and you're finished.

Present ⭐⭐⭐

Box:

❶ Fold in half to make creases and unfold

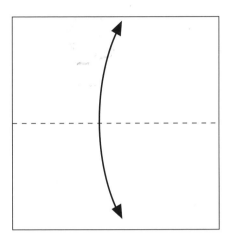

❷ Fold on the dotted lines to make crease and unfold.

❸ Fold on the dotted lines.

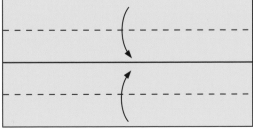

❹ Unfold.

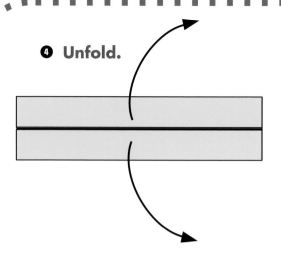

❺ Step fold on the dotted lines.

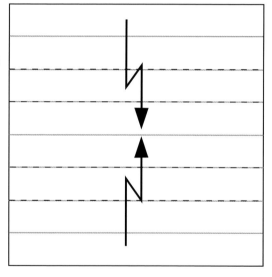

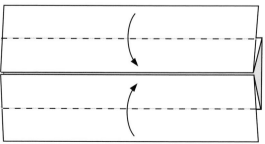

❻ Fold on the dotted lines.

❼ Fold backward on the dotted lines.

❽ Fold on the dotted lines.

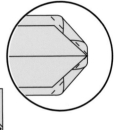

❾ Fold on the dotted lines to make creases and unfold.

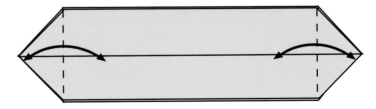

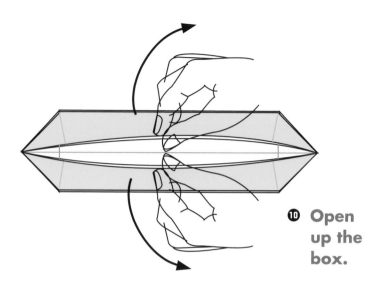

⑩ Open up the box.

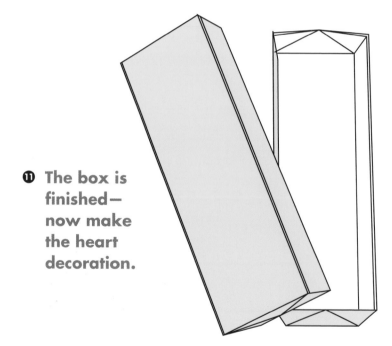

⑪ The box is finished— now make the heart decoration.

Heart Decoration:

(FOLD FROM ¼-SIZE PAPER)

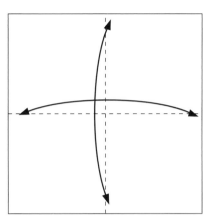

❶ Fold on the dotted lines to make creases and unfold.

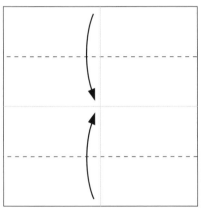

❷ Fold on the dotted lines to meet the center line.

❸ Turn over.

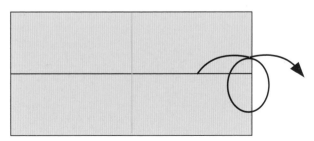

❹ Fold on the dotted lines to meet the center line.

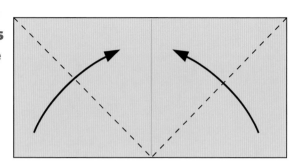

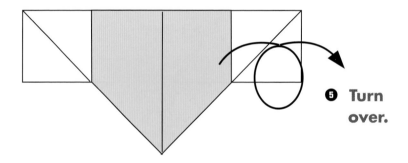

❺ Turn over.

❻ Fold on the dotted line.

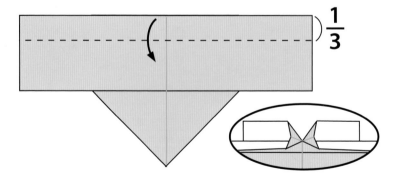

$\dfrac{1}{3}$

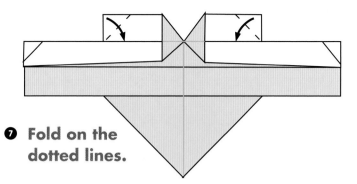

❼ Fold on the dotted lines.

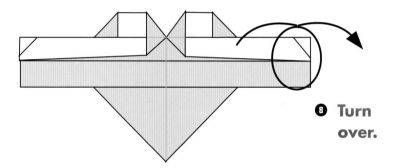

❽ Turn over.

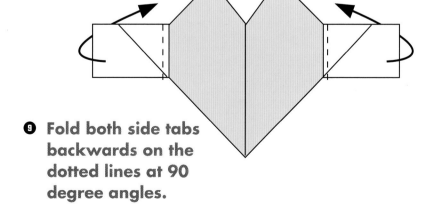

❾ Fold both side tabs backwards on the dotted lines at 90 degree angles.

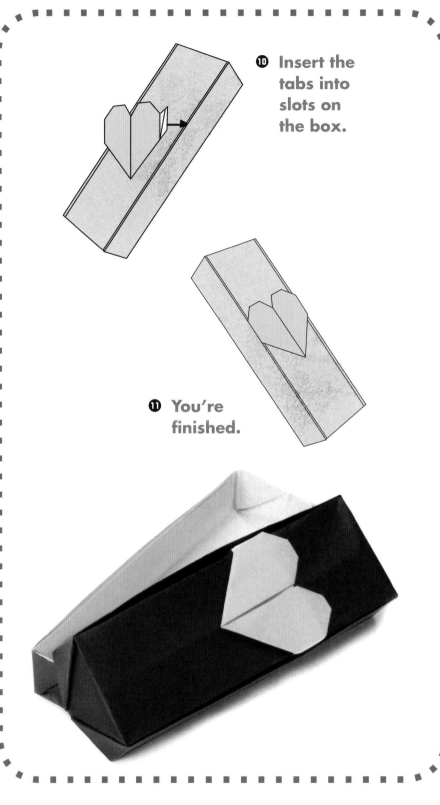

❿ Insert the tabs into slots on the box.

⓫ You're finished.

HALLOWEEN

Witch & Broom

Broom:

1 Fold on the dotted lines to make creases and unfold.

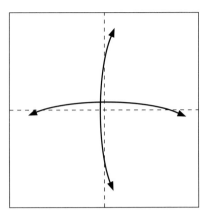

2 Cut with a pair of scissors.

3 Fold in half to make a crease and unfold.

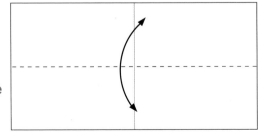

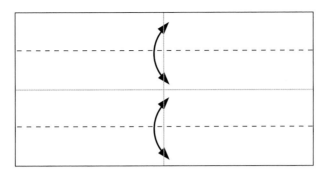

4 Fold on the dotted lines to make creases and unfold.

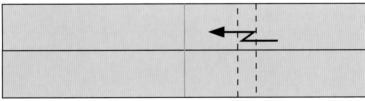

5 Step fold on the dotted lines.

6 Fold on the dotted lines to make creases and unfold.

$\frac{1}{3}$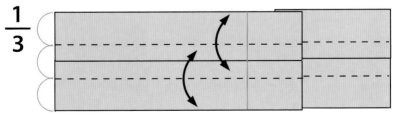

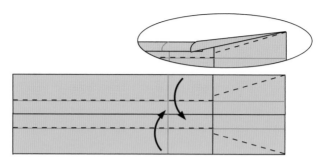

❼ Fold on the
dotted lines.

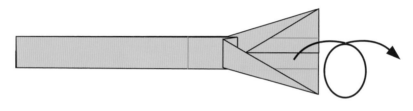

❽ Turn
over.

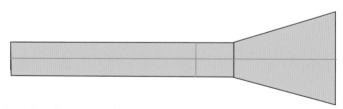

❾ The broom is
finished—now
you need to
make the witch.

Witch:

❶ Fold on the dotted lines to meet the center line.

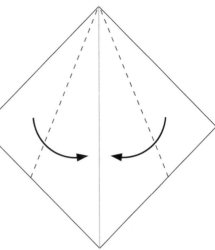

❷ Fold in half to make a crease and fold.

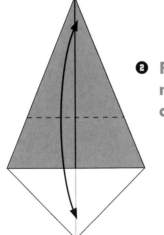

❸ Fold on the dotted line.

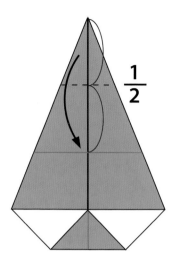

❹ Fold to make a
crease and fold.

❺ Fold on the
dotted lines.

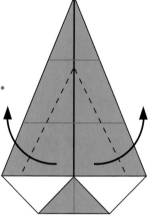

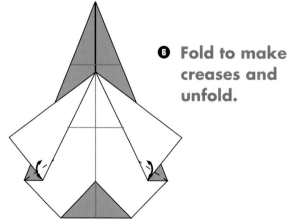

❻ Fold to make
creases and
unfold.

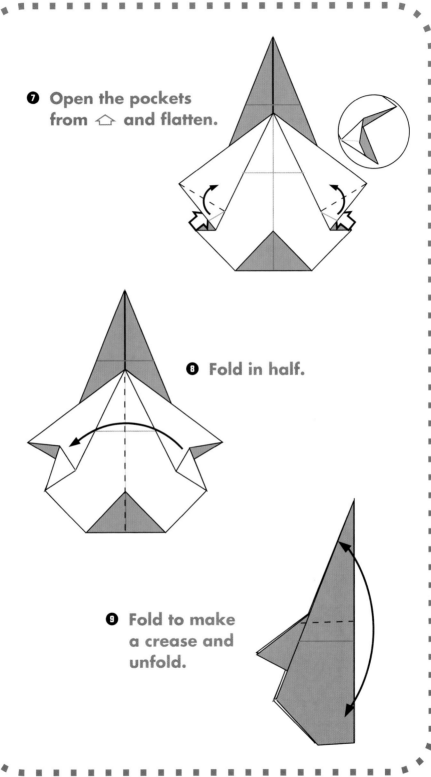

❼ Open the pockets from 🏠 and flatten.

❽ Fold in half.

❾ Fold to make a crease and unfold.

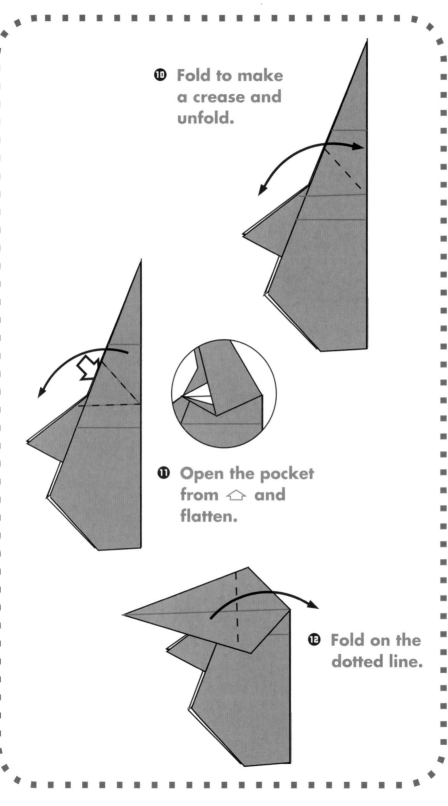

⑩ Fold to make a crease and unfold.

⑪ Open the pocket from ⬆ and flatten.

⑫ Fold on the dotted line.

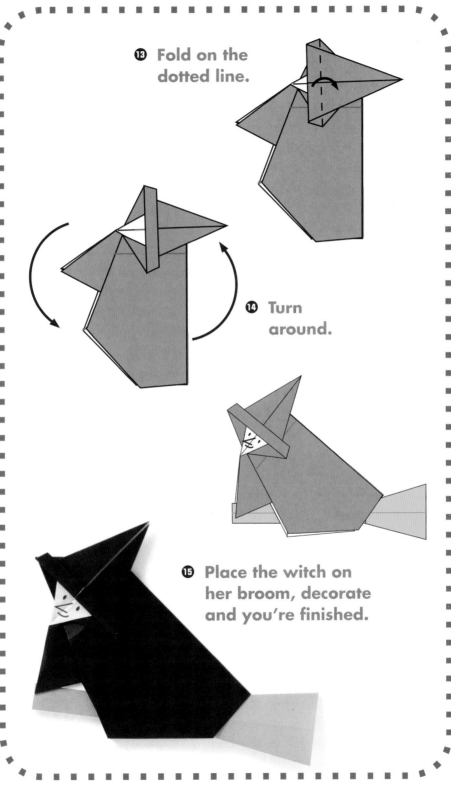

⓭ Fold on the dotted line.

⓮ Turn around.

⓯ Place the witch on her broom, decorate and you're finished.

Bat ★★★

❶ Fold in half to make a crease and unfold.

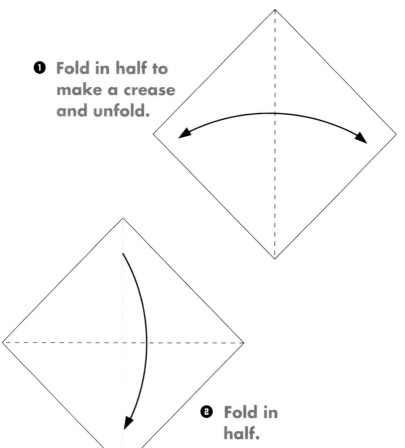

❷ Fold in half.

❸ Fold backward on the dotted line.

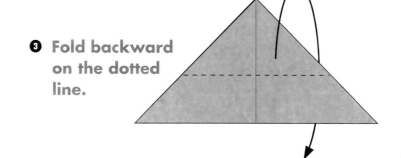

❹ Step fold on
the dotted
lines.

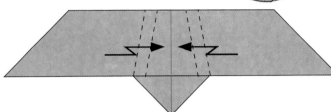

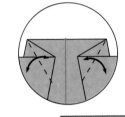

❺ Fold on the dotted
lines to make
creases and unfold.

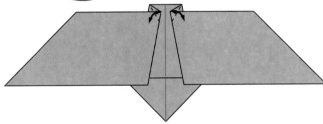

❻ Turn
over.

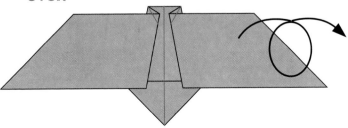

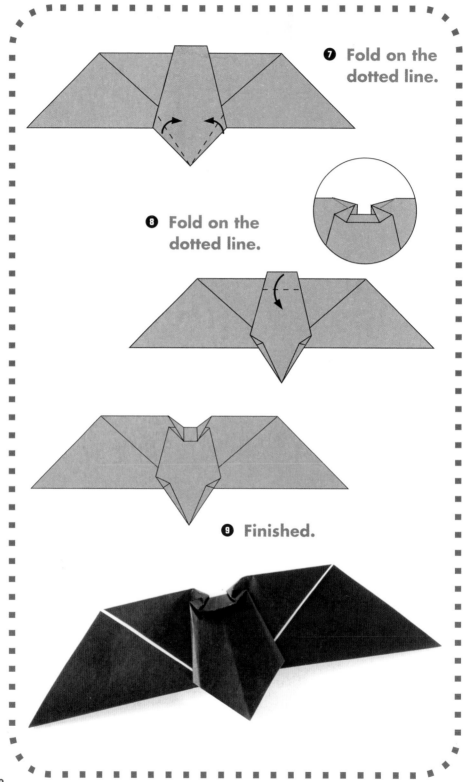

7 Fold on the dotted line.

8 Fold on the dotted line.

9 Finished.

Index